CLEAN
SNACKS

Paleo Vegan Recipes with Keto Options

CLEAN SNACKS

ARMAN LIEW

The Countryman Press
A division of W. W. Norton & Company
Independent Publishers Since 1923

For information about permission to reproduce selections from this book, write to Permissions,
The Countryman Press, 500 Fifth Avenue, New York, NY 10110

For information about special discounts for bulk purchases, please contact
W. W. Norton Special Sales at specialsales@wwnorton.com or 800-233-4830

Manufacturing by RR Donnelley, Shenzhen
Production manager: Devon Zahn

Library of Congress Cataloging-in-Publication Data

Names: Liew, Arman, author.
Title: Clean snacks : Paleo vegan recipes with keto options / Arman Liew.
Description: New York, NY : Countryman Press, a division of W. W. Norton & Company
Independent Publishers Since, 1923, [2019] | Includes bibliographical references and index.
Identifiers: LCCN 2019002488 | ISBN 9781682683194 (hardcover : alk. paper)
Subjects: LCSH: Vegan cooking. | High-protein diet—Recipes. | LCGFT: Cookbooks.
Classification: LCC TX837 .L479 2019 | DDC 641.5/6362—dc23
LC record available at https://lccn.loc.gov/2019002488

The Countryman Press
www.countrymanpress.com

A division of W. W. Norton & Company, Inc.
500 Fifth Avenue, New York, NY 10110
www.wwnorton.com

10 9 8 7 6 5 4 3 2 1

NUTRITIONAL DISCLAIMER

Please note that I possess no official certifications in nutrition, fitness, or the health industry. I include basic nutritional information in these recipes, and base the nutritional value on the ingredients I use. Using different ingredients or different brands from those used in the recipes will alter the recipe's nutritional content. If you follow a strict calorie-controlled or macronutrient-specific diet, it would be in your best interest to double check each recipe's Nutritional Information calculations to your own needs.

For anything medical or nutrition related, please contact a medical professional or certified dietician.

CONTENTS

INTRODUCTION

I CAN'T BELIEVE IT HAS BEEN over a year since my first cookbook, *Clean Sweets*, was released.

One year after that release, the cookbook bug came back in full force and we stand here today with book number two!

Over the last two years, *The Big Man's World* (thebigmansworld.com) has matured and taken a more direct approach on recipes and content. My recipes were originally focused on paleo/gluten-free recieps with vegan options. Now I make a concerted effort to ensure that my recipes fit both dietary lifestyles in their initial form—no options needed! While continuing to share recipes regularly has never changed, something else did: I got to actively engage with you, the loyal reader.

Through our daily (sometimes hourly) interactions on social media, I've been able to share my life with you, not just in the kitchen, but outside of it too. Because of our regular communication, banter, and questions, I've been able to tailor *Clean Snacks* to *truly* satisfy the cravings most of you have!

Being on *one* sort of diet is already hard enough, but what happens when you throw others into the mix too? What happens if you are in a family or friendship group where one person is paleo, one person is strictly vegan, and the other has celiac disease?

These are just added stresses no one needs.

Let me take the stress off you. Let me help you make recipes that fit paleo, vegan, AND gluten-free diets. Let these recipes encourage you to use healthy, wholesome ingredients that taste delicious and make you feel great. Let these recipes help your meals be easy, adaptable, and full of variety.

PALEO, VEGAN, *AND* GLUTEN-FREE?

YES, FRIENDS.

You asked, I listened.

No more separate snacks for those who follow a paleo diet, those who follow a vegan diet, and those who follow a gluten-free diet.

Every single recipe (apart from the bonus recipes in the keto chapter) are 100 percent vegan, gluten-free, paleo, and grain-free. They have been tested (multiple times!) on my friends and all the recipes were approved!

I've tried my best to call for the same ingredients in multiple recipes, so you can use those standard ingredients over and over again.

Please read each recipe carefully for notes and tips. I sometimes provide ingredient alternatives and even easy swaps that you can use to adapt a recipe to suit your particular dietary needs.

But there is more!

As mentioned earlier, there is a *keto chapter!*

It has been such an exciting year. I've learned so much about the ketogenic diet, and a plethora of my readers have found great success with this diet. The ketogenic diet, in a very simplified form, is an extremely low-carb diet, which puts the dieter in ketosis. This is the process of the liver producing ketones that the body uses to burn energy. Therefore, I've included a dozen 100 percent ketogenic snack recipes. Now you can always have keto snacks on hand when you want to keep those net carbs low!

A GUIDE TO ALTERNATIVE INGREDIENTS

Unless you are considering aspartame or liquid stevia, you are generally safe to swap out any granulated sweetener of choice in recipes.

- **Coconut Palm Sugar:** My preferred sweetener. It does not taste like coconut, irrespective of its name. It is dark in color and isn't overly sweet.

- **Table Sugar:** If sugar isn't an issue for you, it's the stock-standard choice.

- **Granulated Sucralose:** The best zero-calorie sweetener for any recipe, as it doesn't lose sweetness when baked, and also doesn't leave any bitter aftertastes.

- **Granulated Aspartame:** A less-superior version of sucralose, aspartame does not work well with baked goods—it loses its sweetness at higher temperatures.

- **Liquid Stevia:** I'd recommend using liquid stevia as an addition to a granulated sweetener; I try not to use it in my own recipes, as most brands I've tried turn out to be slightly bitter or overly sweet. Saying that, it generally bakes well, and a little goes a long way.

- **Granulated Stevia:** Similar to liquid stevia, but I've yet to find a granulated stevia that doesn't leave a bitter aftertaste. I know many people find brands that work well for them, so feel free to do so. This bakes well and does not lose its sweetness at high temperature.

- **Monk Fruit Sweetener:** This is my favorite keto, paleo, and vegan-friendly sweetener. It leaves no bitter aftertaste and works well in both baked and non-baked recipes.

MILK ALTERNATIVES

You'll notice most recipes call for a "milk of choice." As long as it's not canned coconut milk (or condensed milk!) you can use any milk you have on hand—they will all produce a similar result. Besides cow's milk, here are the other three varieties I recommend and use most often.

- **Unsweetened Almond Milk:** Easy, convenient, and virtually flavorless, it adds a natural creaminess to oatmeal and smoothies.

- **Coconut Milk:** Unsweetened coconut milk is similar to unsweetened almond milk. It doesn't have a distinct coconut flavor, and is relatively low-fat.

- **Soy Milk/Rice Milk/Oat Milk:** I wouldn't recommend these for beverages or frozen recipes, as they tend to be a little thin. They work fine in baked goods and mug cakes.

MAKE YOUR OWN FLAX EGG

Flax eggs are the most versatile egg substitute in recipes. I've found that the way you make a flax egg can really make an impact on the final result. My personal favorite method may be a little more time consuming, but I find it is the most accurate resemblance to an egg in recipes. It also has a milder taste.

This may seem more time consuming than packaged flax eggs but it lends a much better texture to your finished product.

PERFECT FLAX EGG

Makes 1 flax egg

INGREDIENTS

3 tablespoons cold water

1 tablespoon whole flax seeds

Blend your whole flax seeds into a fine powder. In a small bowl, combine the powder with cold water and refrigerate the mixture for at least 30 minutes.

HEALTHY
BAKED SNACKS

ORANGE COCONUT MACAROONS

The coconut and citrus combination is one of my favorites—I love the subtle tang of citrus mixed with the sweetness of coconut. If you're not a fan of orange, you can easily replace the orange juice and zest with lemon!

Yield: 20 macaroons | **Total Time:** 15 minutes

NUTRITIONAL INFORMATION PER MACAROON

Calories 119, Protein 1 gram, Fat 10 grams, Fiber 1 gram, Carbs 8 grams

2½ cups finely shredded coconut (macaroon or desiccated coconut), plus more for sprinkling

½ cup almond flour (I use blanched almond flour)

⅓ cup coconut oil

½ cup pure maple syrup (can sub for agave nectar)

2 tablespoons orange juice

¼ cup orange zest, plus more for sprinkling

Macaroons can be stored at room temperature, in an airtight container for up to 1 week. They can also be refrigerated, and they freeze well.

1. Preheat the oven to 350°F (180°C). Line and grease a large baking tray with parchment paper or aluminum tin foil and set aside.

2. In a high-speed blender or food processor, combine all the ingredients and pulse until a thick dough remains. Scrape down the sides regularly to avoid clumps of coconut forming.

3. Using a cookie scoop or large circular spoon, drop balls of the coconut mixture on the lined baking tray, ensuring that they are around an inch or two apart.

4. Bake for 15 to 20 minutes, or until golden around the edges and golden on top. Remove from oven. Sprinkle extra zest and coconut on top then allow to cool on the tray for 10 minutes before transferring to a wire rack to cool completely.

CHOCOLATE CHIP BLONDIES

These chocolate chip blondies are one of my "go-to" desserts. They impress even my nonvegan friends! Tip: Warm them up slightly before serving so the chocolate chips melt.

Yield: 12 bars | **Total Time:** 20–25 minutes

NUTRITIONAL INFORMATION PER BAR

Calories 146, Protein 5 grams, Fat 20 grams, Fiber 2 grams, Carbs 25 grams

1 flax egg (see note)

1 cup granulated sweetener of choice

½ cup nut or seed butter of choice (I use almond butter)

1 cup almond flour

2 tablespoons coconut flour

1 teaspoon vanilla extract

¼ cup nondairy milk of choice (I use unsweetened almond milk)

¼ cup nondairy chocolate chips of choice

If you do not follow a vegan diet, you can replace the flax egg with one whole egg.

Blondies can keep at room temperature, in a sealed container, for up to 3 days. For optimum freshness, keep bars refrigerated.

1. Preheat the oven to 350°F (180°C). Line an 8-inch square pan with parchment paper and set aside.

2. In a large mixing bowl, combine all the ingredients, except the milk and chocolate chips. Mix until a crumbly texture remains.

3. Add the milk and mix until a dough remains. Stir through the chocolate chips and transfer batter to the lined pan.

4. Bake for 20 to 25 minutes until golden on the edges and on top or until a skewer comes out clean from the center. Allow to cool in the pan for 10 minutes before transferring to a wire rack to cool completely. Once cool, cut into 12 bars.

CLASSIC CHOCOLATE MUG CAKE

Satisfy your chocolate and cake cravings in one dessert! This single-serving cake is perfectly loaded with chocolate, and it tastes even better with an added scoop of ice cream. Don't have a microwave? Check out the oven instructions.

Yield: 1 cake | **Total Time:** 15 minutes

NUTRITIONAL INFORMATION
Calories 169, Protein 7 grams, Fat 10 grams, Fiber 9 grams, Carbs 19 grams

2 tablespoons cocoa powder

1 tablespoon coconut flour

1 tablespoon granulated sweetener of choice

¼ teaspoon baking powder

1 tablespoon almond butter (can sub for any nut or seed butter)

3 tablespoons mashed banana (can sub for mashed sweet potato or pumpkin)

1–2 tablespoons nondairy milk of choice

1 tablespoon nondairy chocolate chips (optional)

To make in the oven, preheat to 350°F (180°C) and grease an oven-safe 6-inch ramekin. Bake for 10 to 12 minutes, but check around the 8-minute mark if you want an ultra-gooey chocolate cake.

1. In a small microwave-safe bowl or mug, add the dry ingredients and mix well.

2. Add the almond butter and mashed banana and mix well. Add 1 tablespoon of milk until a thick, gooey batter remains. If the batter is a little too dry, add an extra tablespoon.

3. Sprinkle with chocolate chips, if using, and microwave for 50 seconds to 2 minutes, and enjoy!

SOFT AND CHEWY CHOCOLATE CHIP COOKIES

The classic chocolate chip cookie has been given a healthy and low-sugar makeover. No grains and no eggs—no kidding! These soft and chewy cookies are ready in under 20 minutes.

Yield: 12 cookies | **Total Time:** 12–15 minutes

NUTRITIONAL INFORMATION PER COOKIE

Calories 170, Protein 4 grams, Fat 14 grams, Fiber 3 grams, Carbs 12 grams

1½ cups almond flour (I use blanched almond flour)

3 tablespoons coconut flour

1 teaspoon baking powder

¼ cup coconut oil, melted

¼ cup pure maple syrup (can sub for agave nectar)

2 tablespoons unsweetened applesauce

¼ cup nondairy chocolate chips

The cookies will not spread much as they bake. Be sure to flatten them appropriately, otherwise you will be left with ball-shaped cookies.

These cookies can be kept at room temperature in an airtight container for up to 5 days. They are also freezer friendly and keep for up to 1 month.

1. Preheat the oven to 350°F (180°C). Line a large baking tray or cookie sheet with parchment paper and set aside.

2. In a large mixing bowl, combine the dry ingredients and mix well.

3. In a separate bowl, mix the melted coconut oil with the maple syrup. Add the applesauce and whisk until a thick liquid is formed. Pour into the dry mixture and mix very well, until a thick dough is formed. Stir the chocolate chips through the dough.

4. Using your hands, form small balls with the dough. Place the balls of dough onto the lined baking tray, and using the palms of your hands flatten each ball into a cookie shape.

5. Bake the cookies for 10 to 12 minutes, until the edges become golden brown. Remove from the oven and allow to cool on the pan for 10 minutes before transferring to a wire rack to cool completely.

FLOURLESS ALMOND BUTTER COOKIES

These foolproof cookies are made with just four ingredients. For those who don't follow a vegan diet, feel free to swap out the chia seeds with a whole egg.

Yield: 12 cookies | **Total Time:** 12–15 minutes

NUTRITIONAL INFORMATION PER COOKIE

Calories 155, Protein 18 grams, Fat 13 grams, Fiber 4 grams, Carbs 18 grams

1 cup smooth almond butter (can sub for any nut or seed butter)

¾ cup granulated sweetener of choice (I use erythritol)

3–4 tablespoons ground chia seeds (see note)

¼ cup crushed nuts of choice (optional)

For a nonvegan alternative, a whole egg can be substituted for the ground chia seeds.

These cookies can keep in a sealed container for up to a week.

1. Preheat the oven to 350°F (180°C) and line a large baking tray or cookie sheet with parchment paper and set aside.

2. In a large mixing bowl, combine the almond butter, sweetener, and 3 tablespoons of the chia seeds. If the batter is too thin, add the extra tablespoon of chia seeds.

3. Using a cookie scoop or your hands, form small balls and place them on the baking tray, 3 to 4 inches apart. Press each ball into a cookie shape and top with crushed nuts, if using. Bake for 8 to 12 minutes, or until the cookies are "just" cooked and golden brown. Remove from the oven and allow to cool until soft, firm, and chewy.

FLOURLESS CHOCOLATE BLENDER MUFFINS

These flourless chocolate muffins are the ultimate chocolate fix. They are made in one bowl or one blender. To take it up a notch, heat slightly before eating so that the chocolate chips melt into it!

Yield: 12 muffins | **Total Time:** 25–30 minutes (see note)

NUTRITIONAL INFORMATION PER MUFFIN

Calories 187, Protein 5 grams, Fat 12 grams, Fiber 4 grams, Carbs 16 grams

1 cup smooth almond butter (can sub for any nut or seed butter)

1 cup unsweetened applesauce (can sub for pumpkin or banana)

½ cup pure maple syrup (can sub for agave nectar)

½ cup cocoa powder

1 teaspoon baking powder

¼ cup granulated sweetener of choice (see note)

½ cup nondairy chocolate chips of choice (optional)

Only add the granulated sweetener if you prefer a sweeter muffin.

Cooking times may vary depending on whether you use applesauce, banana, or pumpkin.

If you don't have a high-speed blender, you can use a large mixing bowl. Just ensure the batter is smooth before baking.

Muffins should be kept refrigerated, and can keep for up to 5 days.

1. Preheat the oven to 350°F (180°C). Grease a 12-count muffin tin or silicone muffin pan and set aside.

2. In a high-speed blender, combine all the ingredients, except chocolate chips, and pulse until a smooth batter remains. Regularly scrape down the sides. Stir through the chocolate chips, if using.

3. Distribute the muffin batter evenly between the muffin tin cups. Bake for 20 to 30 minutes, or until a skewer comes out clean from the center.

4. Let the muffins cool in the pan for 15 minutes before transferring to a wire rack to cool completely.

FLOURLESS CHOCOLATE CHIP BANANA BREAD

Everyone needs a classic banana bread recipe in their repertoire. This one tastes better when chocolate chips are added in. Moist and tender, this perfect baked treat will be among your favorites!

Yield: 12–15 slices | **Total Time:** 45–50 minutes

NUTRITIONAL INFORMATION PER SLICE

Calories 249, Protein 5 grams, Fat 22 grams, Fiber 3 grams, Carbs 15 grams

2 cups almond flour

2 tablespoons granulated sweetener of choice (optional, only if you prefer a sweeter banana bread)

1 teaspoon baking powder

1 teaspoon cinnamon

¼ teaspoon salt

½ cup coconut oil, melted

2 large, overripe bananas, mashed (see note)

2 flax eggs (can sub for whole eggs, if not strictly vegan)

1 teaspoon vanilla extract

½ cup nondairy chocolate chips

If your batter seems a little on the drier side, add extra banana or some liquid of choice (nondairy milk or maple syrup).

If you use a square pan, cooking time will be less than when using a traditional loaf pan.

Banana bread can be kept refrigerated for up to a week. It is freezer friendly and can keep for up to 2 months.

1. Preheat the oven to 350°F (180°C). Grease an 8-inch loaf pan or 10-inch square pan (see note) and set aside.

2. In a large mixing bowl, add the dry ingredients and mix well.

3. In a separate medium bowl, add the melted coconut oil. Add the mashed bananas, flax eggs, and vanilla, and whisk together.

4. Combine the wet and dry ingredients and mix until fully incorporated. Stir through the chocolate chips.

5. Pour the banana bread batter into the greased pan and bake for 40 to 50 minutes (check around the 40-minute mark), or until a toothpick comes out clean from the center.

6. Let cool in the pan for 10 minutes before transferring to a wire rack to cool completely.

CLASSIC BANANA
BREAD MUFFINS

Banana bread muffins are a great way to use up those leftover bananas, and this one is made with no grains and no eggs!

Yield: 12 muffins | **Total Time:** 25–30 minutes

NUTRITIONAL INFORMATION PER MUFFIN

Calories 205, Protein 4 grams, Fat 19 grams, Fiber 3 grams, Carbs 9 grams

2 cups almond flour

2 tablespoons granulated sweetener of choice (optional, only if you prefer a sweeter banana bread)

1 teaspoon baking powder

1 teaspoon cinnamon

¼ teaspoon salt

½ cup coconut oil, melted

2–3 large, overripe bananas, mashed, plus more if needed

2 flax eggs (can sub for whole eggs, if not strictly vegan)

1 teaspoon vanilla extract

Muffins can keep at room temperature for up to 3 days. They are best kept refrigerated, but they are also freezer friendly.

1. Preheat the oven to 350°F (180°C). Grease a 12-count muffin tin or silicone muffin pan and set aside.

2. In a large mixing bowl, add the dry ingredients and mix well.

3. In a separate medium-sized bowl, add the melted coconut oil. Add the mashed bananas, flax eggs, and vanilla, and whisk together.

4. Combine your wet and dry ingredients and mix until fully incorporated. If your batter is too thick or crumbly, add extra banana *or* a liquid of choice (nondairy milk or pure maple syrup). Divide evenly among the muffin tin cups.

5. Bake for 20 to 30 minutes, or until a toothpick comes out clean from the center.

6. Let cool in the pan for 5 minutes before transferring to a wire rack to cool completely.

FLUFFY PANCAKES

These delicious fluffy pancakes are made with no eggs and no dairy. They are perfect when layered with your favorite toppings!

Yield: 4 servings | **Total Time:** 10 minutes

1 cup almond flour, plus more if needed

6 tablespoons tapioca flour

1 teaspoon cinnamon

1 tablespoon baking powder

Pinch sea salt

½ cup + 2 tablespoons coconut milk, plus more if needed

1 teaspoon apple cider vinegar (can use lemon juice or lime juice)

1 tablespoon pure maple syrup

1 tablespoon coconut oil, melted

Pancake batter can be made in a blender instead of a mixing bowl.

Pancakes are freezer friendly and perfect for quick grab-and-go breakfasts!

1. In a large mixing bowl, add the dry ingredients and mix well.

2. Add the remaining ingredients and mix very well, regularly scraping down the sides to ensure all the batter is fully incorporated. If the batter is too thick, add some extra coconut milk as needed. If the batter is too thin, add a little extra almond flour.

3. On medium heat, preheat a greased pan. When hot, add ¼ cup portions of the pancake batter. Cook for 1 to 2 minutes, or until bubbles form around the edges before flipping and cooking for an extra 1 to 2 minutes.

4. Repeat until all pancakes are done. Top as desired, or layer with peanut butter and jam!

HEALTHY SAVORY SNACKS

CREAMY AVOCADO DIP

This versatile avocado dip is made with just four ingredients. Use it as a dip for crackers, stir it through pasta, or even use it as a sandwich spread!

Yield: 4 servings | **Total Time:** 5 minutes

NUTRITIONAL INFORMATION PER SERVING

Calories 117, Protein 2 grams, Fat 11 grams, Fiber 5 grams, Carbs 6 grams

2 medium avocados

1½ teaspoons lemon juice

¼ teaspoon red pepper flakes

Salt and pepper, to taste

Feel free to add any extra spices or herbs.

Creamy avocado dip should be kept refrigerated, and can keep for 3 days.

In a high-speed blender or food processor, blend all your ingredients until thick and creamy.

CREAMY BEET DIP

Sweet, salty, and seriously addictive, you'll have trouble not digging into this dip with a spoon. You won't believe how creamy it is even though there's no dairy or butter!

Yield: 16 servings | **Total Time:** 5 minutes

NUTRITIONAL INFORMATION PER SERVING

Calories 136, Protein 4 grams, Fat 12 grams, Fiber 3 grams, Carbs 4 grams

1½ cups blanched almonds, soaked for 45 minutes (can sub for raw cashews)

1 large beet, steamed and cooled completely (see note)

¼ cup + 1 tablespoon lemon juice

¼ cup liquid of choice (water or nondairy milk)

3 tablespoons olive oil (can sub for any neutral-tasting oil, like avocado)

¼ cup tahini (can sub for almond butter or a seed butter)

1 teaspoon cayenne pepper

Salt and pepper, to taste

1 tablespoon pine nuts (optional)

You can use packaged precooked beet, but the flavor will be more sour and the texture will be a little more gritty.

Beet dip can keep in the refrigerator for a week, in a sealed container.

1. In a high-speed blender or food processor, add the soaked almonds (remove water) and blend for 20 seconds. Add all the other ingredients except the pine nuts and blend until thick and creamy.

2. If the dip is too thick, add extra olive oil and continue to pulse.

3. Transfer to a large bowl, top with pine nuts, if using, and serve.

SECRET INGREDIENT HUMMUS

I've never been a huge fan of chickpeas, but I have always loved hummus. I'd been meaning to create alternatives that taste like a classic hummus, minus the legumes. And here it is!

Yield: 12 servings | **Total Time:** 20 minutes

NUTRITIONAL INFORMATION PER SERVING

Calories 60, Protein 2 grams, Fat 5 grams, Fiber 1 gram, Carbs 2 grams

1 large red pepper, halved and core removed

Sea salt, to taste

1½ cups zucchini, peeled and chopped

¼ cup tahini (can sub for any nut or seed butter)

2 tablespoons olive oil (can sub for any neutral-tasting oil, like avocado), plus more if needed

1 tablespoon lemon juice

2 cloves garlic

1 teaspoon mixed spice (can sub for cumin or garam masala)

Salt and pepper, to taste

1 teaspoon cayenne pepper, plus more to garnish

Feel free to add any extra spices or herbs to it.

The hummus should be kept refrigerated, and can keep for 5 days.

1. Preheat the oven to 350°F (180°C). Line a baking tray with parchment paper and set aside.

2. Place the pepper skin-side up on the tray. Bake for 15 to 20 minutes, or until the skin starts to char. Remove from the oven and let cool completely.

3. Sprinkle sea salt over the zucchini and set aside.

4. Remove the skins from the peppers and cut into pieces. Add to a high-speed blender or food processor, along with the zucchini, and lightly blend.

5. Add all the other ingredients and pulse until thick and creamy. If the dip is too thick, add a little extra olive oil.

6. Transfer to a large bowl and top with extra cayenne pepper and serve immediately.

SPICED BAKED POTATO WEDGES

A perfect veggie-packed side dish or savory snack on its own, these four-ingredient baked potato wedges have you covered!

Yield: 4 servings as a side dish | **Total Time:** 40 minutes

NUTRITIONAL INFORMATION PER SERVING

Calories 141, Protein 3 grams, Fat 4 grams, Fiber 2 grams, Carbs 26 grams

4 medium potatoes, washed and sliced into wedges

1 tablespoon avocado oil

½ teaspoon basil (can sub for mixed herbs)

Salt and pepper, to taste

Feel free to add any extra spices or herbs.

1. Preheat the oven to 400°F (200°C). Line a large baking tray with parchment paper and set aside.

2. In a large mixing bowl, add the sliced potatoes and drizzle oil over the top. Add the herbs and seasonings and mix very well, until combined.

3. Spread the potatoes in a single layer and bake for 35 to 40 minutes, or until crispy and golden.

BAKED CURLY FRIES

For a fun and tasty way to enjoy potatoes, these low-fat and perfectly seasoned baked curly fries are your answer. Don't own a spiralizer? A veggie peeler works just as well!

Yield: 4 small servings | **Total Time:** 5 minutes

NUTRITIONAL INFORMATION PER SERVING

Calories 68, Protein 2 grams, Fat 1 gram, Fiber 1 gram, Carbs 13 grams

¼ teaspoon garlic powder
¼ teaspoon onion powder
Salt and pepper, to taste
2 large russet potatoes
Cooking spray, to coat

Feel free to add any extra spices or herbs.

If there are still undercooked fries, cook those separately after removing the already-cooked fries.

1. Preheat the oven to 425°(210°C)F. Line a large baking tray with parchment paper and set aside.

2. In a small bowl, combine the spices and set aside.

3. Spiralize the potatoes in a large mixing bowl. Using kitchen scissors, cut the fries into 5- to 7-inch lengths so they do not tangle and can cook evenly.

4. Spread the fries evenly on the tray, ensuring they are separated to avoid them becoming soggy. Spray lightly with cooking spray. Bake for 15 minutes, then mix the fries around and turn over to cook evenly. Bake until crispy and golden, about 10 minutes.

5. Serve immediately with your favourite condiments.

BAKED VEGGIE CHIPS

This colorful savory snack uses up all those delicious root vegetables. Ready in under 45 minutes, they can be seasoned any way you like.

Yield: 4 servings | **Total time:** 5 minutes

NUTRITIONAL INFORMATION PER SERVING

Calories 63, Protein 1 gram, Fat 4 grams, Fiber 3 grams, Carbs 8

1 medium golden beet
1 medium beet
1 large carrot
1 large sweet potato
1 medium turnip
1 tablespoon avocado oil
Salt and pepper, to taste

You can change up any of the root vegetables, but be aware that cooking times will differ. Sweet potatoes will need a longer cooking time versus beets.

1. Preheat the oven to 400°F (200°C). Line a large baking tray with parchment paper and set aside.

2. Using a mandoline or knife, slice the root vegetables into thin slices. Place them into a large mixing bowl, add the avocado oil and seasonings and mix to coat the vegetables.

3. Spread the vegetables in a single layer, minimizing any overlap. Bake for 10 to 12 minutes, before flipping and baking for another 10 minutes, or until crispy.

4. Remove from the oven and allow to cool completely.

BAKED SWEET POTATO ZUCCHINI TOTS

Veggie skeptics will be converted. These bite-sized, low-carb, high-fiber tots are perfect to dip in your favorite condiments!

Yield: 4 servings | **Total time:** 45 minutes

NUTRITIONAL INFORMATION PER SERVING

Calories 153, Protein 5 grams, Fat 7 grams, Fiber 5 grams, Carbs 19 grams

2 medium sweet potatoes, steamed and cooled

1½ cups finely shredded zucchini (approximately 2 large zucchini)

½ teaspoon red pepper flakes, plus more if needed

½ teaspoon garlic powder, plus more if needed

½ teaspoon onion powder, plus more if needed

Salt and pepper, to taste

½ cup almond flour

For ultra-crispy tots, bake on high heat for the last 2 to 3 minutes.

Tots are freezer friendly, and can keep for up to 1 month.

1. Preheat the oven to 400°F (200°C). Line a large baking tray with parchment paper and set aside.

2. In a large mixing bowl, mash your cooled sweet potatoes.

3. Remove any excess liquid from the shredded zucchini. Add the zucchini to the sweet potatoes. Add the spices and mix very well.

4. In a small mixing bowl, add the almond flour, along with some extra spices. Using your hands, form small tots with the vegetable mixture. Roll the mixture into the almond flour mixture until evenly coated. Arrange on the tray.

5. Bake for 20 minutes before flipping and continuing to bake for an extra 20 minutes, or until golden brown.

6. Cool briefly before enjoying!

SWEET POTATO PIZZA CRUSTS

Veggie-based pizza crusts are super versatile. Top with your favorite toppings and enjoy!

Yield: 4 pizza crusts | **Total time:** 30 minutes

NUTRITIONAL INFORMATION FOR EACH CRUST

Calories 123, Protein 3 grams, Fat 2 grams, Fiber 7 grams, Carbs 23 grams

2 cups baked and mashed sweet potatoes

½ cup coconut flour

¼ cup tapioca starch (can sub for arrowroot powder, if not strictly paleo)

Salt and pepper, to taste

Toppings of choice

Pizza crusts can be prepped in advance and frozen for later consumption. You don't need to bake them twice in the oven—they can be heated in a toaster oven or microwave oven.

1. Combine all the ingredients in a large mixing bowl. Mix/knead well to form a ball of dough. Divide into 4 equal-sized balls. Roll out each of the balls into about half an inch thickness.

2. Coat a large nonstick pan with cooking spray or oil and heat it on the stove on medium heat. Once hot, cook each pizza crust for 4 to 5 minutes before flipping and continuing to cook for an additional 2 to 3 minutes. It will stick slightly at first, but it will loosen up, which is when you know it is ready to flip.

3. Preheat the oven to 400°F (200°C).

4. Top each crust with pizza sauce and toppings of choice. Bake for 10 to 15 minutes, or until the toppings have cooked and the edges of the crust are slightly brown.

5. Cool briefly and slice and enjoy!

TOASTED COCONUT CHIPS

You never have to buy expensive prepackaged coconut chips when you can easily make your own. Mixed into granola, topped on oatmeal, or even made into a trail mix . . . you will find an excuse to add them to everything!

Yield: 2 cups | **Total time:** 10–15 minutes

NUTRITIONAL INFORMATION PER ¾ CUP

Calories 70, Protein 1 gram, Fat 7 grams, Fiber 1 gram, Carbs 4 grams

2 cups unsweetened coconut flakes
1 tablespoon pure maple syrup
Pinch sea salt

Coconut chips can keep in an airtight container for up to 2 weeks.

1. Preheat the oven to 300°F (160°C). Line a large baking sheet with parchment paper and set aside.

2. In a large mixing bowl, combine all the ingredients and mix very well to ensure everything is fully incorporated.

3. Pour the mixture on the tray and bake for 10 to 12 minutes, stirring every 3 to 4 minutes, until golden brown.

4. Allow to cool completely.

NO-BAKE
SNACKS

CHOCOLATE COCONUT BARS

This classic chocolate coconut candy bar has been given a healthy makeover! These seriously addictive bars need just four ingredients, and they satisfy the sweet tooth!

Yield: 16 bars | **Cooking time:** 5–10 minutes

1 cup coconut butter, melted

¼ cup pure maple syrup

2½ cups shredded unsweetened coconut

2–3 cups nondairy chocolate chips of choice (see note)

For a thicker chocolate coating, use around 3 cups of chocolate chips, or drizzle excess melted chocolate over the tops. The recipe uses 2 cups of chocolate chips.

These bars can keep at room temperature, in a sealed container, for up to 2 weeks.

1. Line an 8-inch square pan with parchment paper and set aside.

2. In a small microwave-safe bowl or in a small pan on the stove, combine the coconut butter with maple syrup and mix very well. Alternatively, if the coconut butter is already smooth and creamy, simply whisk with the syrup.

3. Add the coconut and mix very well until fully combined. Pour mixture into the lined pan and press firmly into place. Refrigerate until firm.

4. Use a slightly wet knife and slice into 12 bars. Refrigerate again for at least 30 minutes.

5. In a medium microwave-safe bowl or in a small pan on the stove over low heat, melt the chocolate chips. Remove the coconut bars and, using two forks, dip each bar in the melted chocolate until fully covered. Continue doing so until all the bars are covered in chocolate. Refrigerate until firm.

NO-BAKE FUDGE BARS

Thick, chewy, and fudgy bars topped with a layer of chocolate—yes, please! These bars are super versatile, and the fudge layer can contain any nut or seed butter of your choice.

Yield: 16 bars | **Total time:** 10 minutes

NUTRITIONAL INFORMATION PER BAR

Calories 220, Protein 5 grams, Fat 15 grams, Fiber 3 grams, Carbs 19

1 cup almond butter (can sub for any nut or seed butter)

6 tablespoons pure maple syrup

½ cup coconut flour, plus more if needed

1–2 tablespoons nondairy milk, if needed

1 cup nondairy chocolate chips of choice

These bars should be kept refrigerated at all times, in a sealed container. They can keep for up to a week.

1. Line an 8-inch square pan with parchment paper and set aside.

2. In a small microwave-safe bowl or in a small pan on the stove, combine the almond butter with the maple syrup and heat until melted.

3. Add the coconut flour and whisk into the melted mixture until a thick dough remains. If it is too crumbly, add a little milk. If it is too thin, add some extra coconut flour.

4. Transfer the batter to the pan and press firmly into place. Refrigerate for at least 15 minutes or until firm.

5. In a small microwafe-safe bowl or in a small pan on the stove over low heat, melt the chocolate chips and pour over the tops of the bars. Refrigerate until firm before slicing into bars.

COOKIE DOUGH CUPS

Edible eggless cookie dough covered in a delicious chocolate coating! This is the perfect healthy dessert or something sweet to bring to parties or events!

Yield: 12 cups | **Total time:** 10 minutes

2½ cups nondairy chocolate chips of choice, divided

½ cup blanched almond flour

2 tablespoons coconut flour

2 tablespoons granulated sweetener of choice

2 tablespoons pure maple syrup (can sub for agave nectar)

1½ tablespoons coconut oil, melted

1–2 tablespoons liquid of choice, if needed

Cookie dough cups can keep at room temperature for up to a week. They are best kept refrigerated and are freezer friendly.

1. Line a 12-count muffin tin with muffin liners and set aside.

2. In a small microwafe-safe bowl or in a small pan on the stove over low heat, melt 1½ cups of the chocolate chips. Divide the melted chocolate among the 12 cups, filling each one three-quarters of the way full, scraping down the sides to ensure the muffin liners are all coated in chocolate. Refrigerate for at least 20 minutes, or until the chocolate is firm.

3. Make your cookie dough filling. In a small mixing bowl, add the almond flour, coconut flour, and sweetener.

4. Add the maple syrup and coconut oil and mix very well, until fully combined. The mixture should resemble a creamy cookie dough. Stir through ½ cup of chocolate chips. If the dough is a little too crumbly, stir in some liquid until it becomes smooth.

5. Divide the cookie dough filling evenly among the cups. Melt the remaining ½ cup of chocolate chips and top each muffin cup evenly with it. Refrigerate until firm.

HOMEMADE LOADED NUT BARS

A copycat version of the popular KIND bars, these filling no-bake bars are loaded with nuts and seeds and are sweetened with maple syrup. Feel free to switch up the nuts and seeds used in this recipe!

Yield: 12 bars | **Total time:** 15 minutes

NUTRITIONAL INFORMATION PER BAR

Calories 155, Protein 5 grams, Fat 11 grams, Fiber 3 grams, Carbs 12 grams

1 cup roasted almonds

½ cup mixed nuts of choice (I use cashews and pecans)

3 tablespoons almond flour

3 tablespoons seeds of choice

1 tablespoon flaxseed meal

¼ cup + 2 tablespoons pure maple syrup (can sub for brown rice syrup, if not strictly paleo)

Pinch sea salt

These bars can keep in a sealed container for up to 3 days. They can also be kept refrigerated and are freezer friendly. To keep them from sticking together, wrap each bar in parchment paper individually.

1. Line an 8-inch square pan with parchment paper and set aside.

2. In a large mixing bowl, combine the nuts, almond flour, seeds, and flaxseed meal and mix until combined.

3. In a small microwave-safe bowl or in a small pan on the stove, heat the syrup until melted. Pour over the dry mixture and mix until fully incorporated and the batter is sticky.

4. Transfer the batter to the lined pan and press firmly in place. Sprinkle with sea salt.

5. Refrigerate until firm. Slice into 12 bars.

CHERRY PIE BLISS BARS

Three all-natural ingredients are all you need to make this popular LÄRABAR copycat! For those who are followers of the Whole30 diet plan, these bars are Whole30 compliant too!

Yield: 12 bars | **Total time:** 10 minutes

NUTRITIONAL INFORMATION PER BAR

Calories 135, Protein 3 grams, Fat 6 grams, Fiber 3 grams, Carbs 18 grams

¾ cup pitted Medjool dates, firmly packed

1 cup raw almonds

¾ cup unsweetened dried cherries

I prefer using Medjool dates as they are naturally softer and creamier than traditional dates.

These bars should be kept refrigerated for optimum texture. They can keep for up to a month.

1. If your dates are too firm, allow them to soak in warm water for 10 to 15 minutes.

2. Line an 8-inch square pan or loaf pan with parchment paper and set aside.

3. In a high-spend blender or food processor, add the almonds and blend until a crumbly texture remains.

4. Add the cherries and dates and blend until a thick batter remains. Scrape down the sides of the blender regularly with a spatula to ensure the mixture is fully incorporated. If your batter is still too thick, add a little water or liquid of choice to become softer.

5. Transfer the batter into the lined pan and press firmly into place. Refrigerate until firm and then cut into 12 bars.

RAW BROWNIE BARS

These 100 percent naturally sweetened bars taste like brownies, but are guilt-free! You can switch up the nuts, but I prefer using walnuts and almonds, as they are mild tasting.

Yield: 12 bars | **Total time:** 10 minutes

NUTRITIONAL INFORMATION PER BAR

Calories 139, Protein 3 grams, Fat 6 grams, Fiber 4 grams, Carbs 18 grams

1½ cups + 2 tablespoons pitted Medjool dates, firmly packed

1 cup raw nuts (I use almonds and walnuts)

¼ cup unsweetened cocoa powder

¼ cup nondairy chocolate chips

I prefer using Medjool dates as they are naturally softer and creamier than traditional dates

1. If your dates are too firm, allow to soak in warm water for 10 to 15 minutes.

2. Line an 8-inch square pan or loaf pan with parchment paper and set aside.

3. In a high-spend blender or food processor, add the nuts and blend until a crumbly texture remains.

4. Add the dates and cocoa powder and blend until a thick batter remains. Regularly scrape down the sides with a spatula to ensure the mixture is fully incorporated. If your batter is still too thick, add a little water or liquid of choice to make it softer. Add the chocolate chips and mix through.

5. Transfer the batter into the lined pan and press firmly into place. Refrigerate until firm and then cut into 12 bars.

CLASSIC BLISS BALLS

Bliss balls are the epitome of a quick and easy snack!
Portable, satisfying, and a quick energy fix, they can be altered to suit whatever ingredients you have on hand.

Yield: 16 balls | **Total time:** 15 minutes

NUTRITIONAL INFORMATION
PER BALL
Calories 52, Protein 1 gram, Fat 2 grams, Fiber 2 grams, Carbs 7 grams

¾ cup pitted Medjool dates

½ cup almonds

2 tablespoons cocoa powder, plus more for coating

2 tablespoons shredded coconut, plus more for coating

I prefer using Medjool dates as they are naturally softer and creamier than traditional dates.

Bliss balls don't need to remain refrigerated. They can keep for up to a week in a sealed container.

1. If your dates are too firm, allow to soak in warm water for 10 to 15 minutes.

2. Combine all the ingredients in a high-speed blender or food processor. Pulse well, scraping down the sides to ensure all the ingredients are combined.

3. Pour the dough into a large mixing bowl. Using your hands, form 16 small balls. Roll each ball in extra coconut and cocoa and place on a plate. Refrigerate for 20 minutes to firm up.

DESSERTS

CREAMY CHOCOLATE DIP

Do you have a fruit platter or want something a little sweet to accompany a fancy dessert? This creamy chocolate dip needs just three ingredients and takes minutes to whip up!

Yield: 1¼ cups (6 servings) | **Total time:** 30 minutes

NUTRITIONAL INFORMATION PER SERVING
Calories 102, Protein 1 gram, Fat 9 grams, Fiber 1 gram, Carbs 7 grams

1 cup canned full-fat coconut cream

2 tablespoons pure maple syrup (can sub for agave nectar)

¼ cup cocoa powder

Please do not use coconut milk from a carton, as the consistency is not the same. Light coconut milk will yield a much thinner result—avoid if possible.

Creamy chocolate dip can keep refrigerated for up to a week. If it is too thick, add extra nondairy milk of choice slowly until desired consistency is achieved.

1. In a large mixing bowl, add the coconut cream and maple syrup and mix until well combined.

2. Stir through the cocoa powder and mix very well, until smooth and fully incorporated.

3. Chill for 30 minutes, to thicken.

NEW YORK KETO CHEESECAKE

Making a completely dairy-free cheesecake isn't as difficult as it may seem! This one is thick, creamy, and perfect for a light dessert.

Yield: 12 slices | **Total time** 15 minutes, plus 2 hours to chill

NUTRITIONAL INFORMATION PER SLICE

Calories 293, Protein 8 grams, Fat 28 grams, Fiber 5 grams, Carbs 8 grams, Net Carbs 3 grams

FOR THE CRUST

1½ cups almonds (can use a mix of almonds and cashews)

2 tablespoons coconut oil

1 serving liquid stevia or pure stevia (see note)

FOR THE FILLING

1½ cups cashews, soaked (see note)

⅓ cup coconut milk

1 serving liquid stevia (see note)

⅔ cup coconut oil, melted

3 tablespoons lemon juice

1 teaspoon vanilla extract

Optional toppings

Different brands of liquid stevia have different servings. The one I use is 5 drops = 1 serving. Adjust sweetness accordingly.

For a non-cashew option, you can use blanched almonds. Be sure they are presoaked for easy blending.

This cheesecake should be kept refrigerated, but it is also freezer friendly.

1. Lightly grease a small 6- to 8-inch springform pan.

2. In a high-speed blender or food processor, add all the crust ingredients and blend until a crumbly texture remains. Transfer to the springform pan and press firmly in place. Refrigerate for at least an hour, or until firm.

3. Blend the soaked cashews until an almost buttery texture remains. Add the rest of the filling ingredients except the toppings and blend until smooth and creamy. Regularly scrape down the sides to ensure that all ingredients are fully incorporated.

4. Pour the cheesecake filling onto the chilled crust and refrigerate for 2 hours, or until thick and set. Remove from pan and top with toppings of choice and cut into slices.

SECRET INGREDIENT
CHOCOLATE FROSTING

You won't believe how quick and easy this chocolate frosting is, and it only needs three ingredients. I promise you won't taste the avocado. Cakes, muffins, cupcakes—spread it on everything!

Yield: 1 cup frosting (16 1-tablespoon servings) | **Cooking time** 10 minutes

NUTRITIONAL INFORMATION PER SERVING

Calories 32, Protein 1 gram, Fat 2 grams, Fiber 1 gram, Carbs 5 grams

1 medium-large avocado, peeled and seed removed

¼ cup + 2 tablespoons cocoa powder

¼ cup pure maple syrup (can sub for agave nectar)

Keep leftover frosting in a sealed container, refrigerated, for up to 3 days.

1. In a high-speed blender or food processor, add the avocado and blend until smooth and creamy.

2. Add the cocoa powder and maple syrup and continue blending, until fully incorporated. Regularly scrape down the sides to ensure it is fully mixed.

3. Once thick and glossy, transfer to a bowl and use as frosting!

ALMOND BUTTER
KETO CHOCOLATE MOUSSE

Get ready to grab your spoon and dig into this creamy chocolate mousse made with no dairy and no refined sugar. Bonus? It's also keto-friendly, thanks to the healthy fats.

Yield: 6 small servings | **Total time** 5 minutes

NUTRITIONAL INFORMATION PER SERVING

Calories 225, Protein 5 grams, Fat 21 grams, Fiber 3 grams, Carbs 7 grams

1 (14-ounce) can full-fat coconut cream, chilled

6 tablespoons smooth almond butter (can sub for smooth nut or seed butter)

3 tablespoons cocoa powder

1 teaspoon vanilla extract

1 serving liquid stevia (see note)

Different brands of liquid stevia have different servings. The one I use is 5 drops = 1 serving. Adjust sweetness accordingly.

Chocolate mousse can be refrigerated for up to 1 week.

1. Open the can of chilled coconut cream. Remove the cream layer (solid cream on top of the can) and place in a large mixing bowl. You will not need the liquid portion in the can.

2. Add the almond butter, cocoa powder, vanilla extract, and liquid stevia. Using a stick blender or hand mixer, mix all the ingredients until a smooth batter remains.

3. Refrigerate for 10 to 15 minutes, to thicken. Serve as desired.

FUDGY GOOEY BROWNIES

These classic brownies are better than any boxed mix out there—and they're made with no eggs and no dairy!

Yield: 12 brownies | **Total time** 25–30 minutes

NUTRITIONAL INFORMATION PER BROWNIE

Calories 190, Protein 4 grams, Fat 14 grams, Fiber 4 grams, Carbs 24 grams

¼ cup smooth almond butter (can sub for any smooth nut or seed butter)

6 tablespoons pure maple syrup

¼ cup coconut oil, melted

1 teaspoon almond extract (can sub for vanilla extract)

6 tablespoons granulated sweetener of choice (I use erythritol)

¾ cup unsweetened cocoa powder

½ cup almond flour

Pinch sea salt

2 flax eggs (can sub for 2 whole eggs, if not vegan)

½ cup nondairy chocolate chips of choice

Don't worry if the brownies seem a little undercooked—they will continue to firm up in the pan while cooling.

Brownies should be kept refrigerated in a sealed container. They are also freezer friendly.

1. Preheat the oven to 325°F (175°C). Line an 8-inch square pan with parchment paper and set aside.

2. In a large mixing bowl, combine the almond butter, maple syrup, coconut oil, almond extract, and granulated sweetener. Whisk very well, until a silky, glossy texture remains.

3. Add the remaining ingredients (except for the chocolate chips) and mix very well, until fully incorporated. Scrape down the sides so the mixture is fully combined.

4. Stir through the chocolate chips. Pour the brownie batter into the lined pan and bake for 25 to 30 minutes, or until a toothpick comes out "just clean" from the center. Allow to cool in the pan completely before slicing into 12 pieces.

GRAIN-FREE
GRANOLA CLUSTERS

These chunky granola clusters are made without the need for any oats, eggs, or granulated sugar. This seriously addictive granola is perfect for snacking, breakfast, or topping your favorite yogurt!

Yield: 16 servings | **Total time:** 35 minutes

NUTRITIONAL INFORMATION PER SERVING

Calories 270, Protein 8 grams, Fat 20 grams, Fiber 6 grams, Carbs 17 grams

2 cups unsweetened coconut flakes

3 cups raw unsalted nuts of choice

1 cup almond flour

¼ teaspoon cinnamon

Pinch sea salt

½ cup pure maple syrup

Granola clusters can keep for up to 2 weeks in a sealed container.

1. Preheat the oven to 350°F (180°C). Line a large baking tray with parchment paper and set aside.

2. In a large mixing bowl, add all the dry ingredients and mix well.

3. Add the maple syrup and mix until fully incorporated into the mixture.

4. Transfer to the lined baking tray and spread in an even layer. Bake for 25 to 35 minutes, stirring halfway through.

5. Remove from oven when golden brown on the edges. Allow to cool on the tray completely before breaking apart into clusters.

FROZEN SNACKS

NO-CHURN COFFEE ICE CREAM

You can make naturally sweetened ice cream without an ice cream maker! Simply blend everything together and enjoy it soft serve style—or you can freeze it to scoop out later.

Yield: 2 servings | **Total time** 5 minutes

NUTRITIONAL INFORMATION PER SERVING

Calories 180, Protein 4 grams, Fat 6 grams, Fiber 5 grams, Carbs 30 grams

2–3 medium bananas, frozen and chopped

1–2 tablespoons almond butter (can sub for any nut or seed butter)

1–2 tablespoons unsweetened cocoa powder

1 teaspoon coffee extract

Do not refreeze leftover ice cream. If you do, then reblend it before serving.

1. In a high-speed blender or food processor, add the frozen bananas and blend for 10 seconds to lightly break apart. Add the almond butter, cocoa powder, and coffee extract and blend until combined.

2. Transfer to a bowl to enjoy soft serve style.

3. For a hard-scoop version, place a loaf pan in the freezer. Once ice cream is blended, pour into the loaf pan and place in the freezer. To ensure it doesn't become icy, regularly stir it every 15 to 20 minutes, for the first hour. Before scooping out, thaw for 15 minutes.

NO-CHURN LEMON ICE CREAM

I've never been a huge fan of fruit-flavored ice cream, but this one is an exception—it's a creamy, dairy-free vanilla ice cream with a hint of lemon. Not a fan of citrus? Leave it out completely for an original vanilla ice cream!

Yield: 6 small scoops | **Cooking time** 5 minutes

NUTRITIONAL INFORMATION PER SCOOP

Calories 213, Protein 3 grams, Fat 17 grams, Fiber 1 gram, Carbs 12 grams

1 (14-ounce) can full-fat coconut milk, chilled

¼ cup pure maple syrup

¼ cup cashew butter (can sub for any nut or seed butter)

1 teaspoon vanilla extract

1 teaspoon lemon extract

You can use an ice cream maker if you have one!

1. Place a loaf pan in the freezer.

2. In a high-speed blender, combine all the ingredients and blend until a thick and creamy mixture remains.

3. Pour the ice cream into the loaf pan and freeze for 1 to 2 hours, stirring every 15 to 20 minutes for the first hour to ensure it doesn't become icy.

4. Before scooping out, thaw for 15 minutes.

CHOCOLATE RASPBERRY LAYERED SMOOTHIE

Turn your boring smoothie into something a little more fun—how about a chocolate smoothie topped with a raspberry smoothie? This filling smoothie is a perfect snack or wholesome breakfast meal!

Yield: 2 smoothies | **Total time:** 5 minutes

NUTRITIONAL INFORMATION PER SMOOTHIE

Calories 188, Protein 6 grams, Fat 11 grams, Fiber 8 grams, Carbs 21 grams

1 small frozen banana, divided

1 cup nondairy milk of choice, divided

2 tablespoons almond butter, divided (can sub for any nut or seed butter)

1 tablespoon cocoa powder

½ cup frozen raspberries (see note)

1 tablespoon chia seeds (optional)

You can substitute the raspberries for any berry of choice.

Chia seeds are optional, but include them for an ultra-thick smoothie.

1. In a high-speed blender, add the chocolate layer ingredients: half the frozen banana, half the milk, one tablespoon of the almond butter, and the cocoa powder. Blend and pour into two tall glasses.

2. Rinse the blender and add all remaining ingredients. Blend until thick and creamy, and pour over the chocolate layer!

NO-CHURN RASPBERRY CHIP SORBET

This recipe came about by pure accident when I ran out of milk while making a smoothie. I blended raspberries and added some sweetener and some chocolate chips. And voilà—the perfect frozen sweet treat!

Yield: 2 servings | **Total time** 5 minutes

NUTRITIONAL INFORMATION PER SERVING

Calories 100, Protein 2 grams, Fat 1 gram, Fiber 9 grams, Carbs 24 grams

2 cups frozen raspberries (can use any berry or even mixed berries)

1 tablespoon pure maple syrup (can sub for agave nectar)

1–2 tablespoons nondairy chocolate chips

Do not over-freeze, otherwise you will be left with a rock.

1. Place a small loaf pan or freezer-friendly container in the freezer.

2. In a high-speed blender, combine all the ingredients and blend very well.

3. Pour into the loaf pan. Freeze for 1 to 2 hours, regularly stirring every 15 to 20 minutes for the first hour. Once ready to enjoy, thaw for 15 minutes prior.

CHOCOLATE BROWNIE BATTER SMOOTHIE

Adding a secret ingredient to this smoothie gives it the most amazing texture—it's like a thick brownie batter! It's the perfect excuse to have chocolate for breakfast.

Yield: 1 smoothie | **Total time** 5 minutes

NUTRITIONAL INFORMATION

Calories 242, Protein 7 grams, Fat 21 grams, Fiber 11 grams, Carbs 15 grams

½ cup nondairy milk of choice

½ medium avocado

1–2 tablespoons granulated sweetener of choice

1–2 tablespoons cocoa powder

1 tablespoon almond butter (can sub for any nut or seed butter)

¼ cup ice (optional)

Feel free to add a scoop of your favorite protein powder.

This smoothie isn't overly sweet, so adjust the granulated sweetener (or a liquid sweetener) to suit your taste.

In a high-speed blender, combine all the ingredients and blend until thick and creamy. For an even thicker shake, add ice.

KETO SNACKS

KETO HUMMUS

This creamy hummus substitute is keto-approved and tastes even better than the classic!

Yield: 8 servings | **Total time** 5 minutes

1 medium cauliflower, chopped finely

3–4 garlic cloves

2 tablespoons lemon juice

6 tablespoons tahini

3 tablespoons olive oil (can sub for avocado oil), plus more if needed

¼ teaspoon cumin

Salt and pepper, to taste

Taste during the pulsing to ensure it is salty and spiced enough.

1. In a microwave-safe bowl or in a medium pan on the stove, steam the cauliflower until soft and tender.

2. Drain and place in a food processor or high-speed blender. Add the garlic cloves and blend until a thick purée remains.

3. Add remaining ingredients and pulse until smooth, regularly scraping down the sides. If too thick, add an extra tablespoon of olive oil.

4. Transfer to a bowl and enjoy!

KETO BLUEBERRY MUFFINS

These classic blueberry muffins are made with almond flour, and they're light, fluffy, and almost bakery-like. They're perfectly delicious straight from the oven and are bursting with blueberries!

Yield: 12 muffins | **Total time:** 18–22 minutes

NUTRITIONAL INFORMATION PER MUFFIN

Calories 219, Protein 7 grams, Fat 20 grams, Fiber 6 grams, Carbs 9 grams, Net Carbs 3 grams

2½ cups blanched almond flour

½ cup granulated sweetener of choice

1 teaspoon baking powder

½ teaspoon cinnamon

⅓ cup coconut oil (can sub for butter), melted

⅓ cup coconut milk

1 tablespoon lemon juice

3 large eggs

½ teaspoon almond extract (can sub for vanilla extract)

½–¾ cup blueberries

Do not overbake, as the muffins will become dry and crumbly. Muffins will continue cooking in the pan while cooling.

I don't recommend using almond meal or traditional almond flour, as the texture of the muffins will become slightly more gritty.

Muffins are best kept refrigerated for up to 5 days. They are freezer friendly, and they keep for up to 1 month.

1. Preheat the oven to 350°F (180°C). Line a 12-count muffin tin with muffin liners or a 12-count silicone muffin tray and set aside.

2. In a large mixing bowl, combine the dry ingredients and mix well.

3. In a separate bowl, add the melted coconut oil, coconut milk, lemon juice, eggs, and almond extract and whisk together.

4. Combine the wet and dry ingredients and fold through the blueberries. Evenly distribute the muffin batter among the lined muffin tin cups and bake for 18 to 20 minutes, or until a toothpick comes out clean.

5. Allow to cool for 5 minutes in pan before transferring to a wire rack to cool completely.

KETO CHOCOLATE COOKIES

These easy four-ingredient, grain-free chocolate cookies are super low carb and ready in under 15 minutes!

Yield: 12 cookies | **Total:** 15 minutes

NUTRITIONAL INFORMATION PER COOKIE

Calories 214, Protein 7 grams, Fat 16 grams, Fiber 6 grams, Carbs 8 grams, Net Carbs 2 grams

1¼ cups almond butter (can sub for peanut butter)

6 tablespoons granulated sweetener of choice

½ cup + 2 tablespoons unsweetened cocoa powder

2 large eggs

¼ cup nondairy chocolate chips (optional)

Remove cookies from the oven when "just cooked" as they firm up once cooled.

Cookies can keep in a sealed container for up to 4 days.

1. Preheat the oven to 350°F (180°C). Line a baking tray with parchment paper and set aside.

2. In a large mixing bowl, combine all the ingredients and mix very well. A thick dough should remain.

3. Using your hands, form the dough into 12 balls and place on the lined baking tray. Press each ball into a cookie shape.

4. Bake cookies for 10 to 12 minutes, or until "just cooked." Allow to cool on the tray for 10 minutes before transferring to a wire rack to cool completely.

KETO GUMMY BEARS

Squash your candy cravings and satisfy your sweet tooth with these gelatin-based gummy bears! Have fun playing around with the gummy bear mold!

Yield: 4 servings | **Total time:** 5 minutes

NUTRITIONAL INFORMATION PER SERVING

Calories 29, Protein 6 grams, Fat Trace grams, Fiber Trace grams, Carbs Trace grams, Net Carbs Trace grams

¼ cup gelatin

1 cup water

6 grams sugar-free beverage mix, such as Crystal Light, True Lime, etc.

I use strawberry and lemon flavors, but use any you prefer.

Gummy bears are best kept refrigerated, otherwise they may stick together.

1. In a small microwave-safe bowl or pan, combine the gelatin and water and let sit for 1 to 2 minutes. Stir continuously during this time.

2. Warm the liquid in the microwave, in 30-second intervals, or on the stovetop, stirring every 30 seconds to avoid any clumps forming. Once completely dissolved, add the beverage flavoring and whisk very well.

3. Pour into a gummy bear mold (or even an ice mold) and refrigerate until firm.

KETO GRANOLA BARS

Granola and keto are two words you won't often hear in the same sentence, but these bars will have you saying them together. Perfect for breakfast, a wholesome snack, or a delicious healthy dessert, they totally satisfy!

Yield: 12 bars | **Total time:** 5 minutes

NUTRITIONAL INFORMATION PER BAR

Calories 224, Protein 6 grams, Fat 19 grams, Fiber 6 grams, Carbs 7 grams, Net Carbs 1 gram

½ cup chopped almonds

1 tablespoon chia seeds

6 tablespoons ground flaxseed meal

6 tablespoons mixed seeds

6 tablespoons granulated sweetener of choice

¼ cup shredded coconut

Pinch sea salt

½ cup almond butter (can sub for any nut or seed butter)

¼ cup coconut oil

¼ cup nondairy chocolate chips (optional)

Granola bars can keep at room temperature for up to 3 days. They are best kept refrigerated.

1. Line an 8-inch square tray with parchment paper and set aside.

2. In a large mixing bowl, combine all the dry ingredients and mix well.

3. In a small microwave-safe bowl or pan, combine the almond butter and coconut oil and heat together in the microwave or on the stovetop until melted. Whisk to ensure it is fully incorporated.

4. Pour the wet mixture into the dry mixture and mix very well. Ensure all the ingredients are well combined.

5. Transfer the granola batter to the lined pan and press firmly in place. Refrigerate until firm. Once firm, drizzle with the chocolate chips, if using, and cut into 12 bars.

JUMBO KETO
VANILLA MUG CAKE

Here's your chance to enjoy a perfectly portioned single-serving vanilla mug cake. Made with almond and coconut flour, it's super fluffy and perfect topped with chocolate chips!

Yield: 1 mug cake | **Total time:** 5 minutes

NUTRITIONAL INFORMATION

Calories 347, Protein 10 grams, Fat 26 grams, Fiber 7 grams, Carbs 10 grams, Net Carbs 3 grams

2 tablespoons blanched almond flour

1 tablespoon coconut flour

¼ teaspoon baking powder

1–2 tablespoons granulated sweetener of choice

½ teaspoon cinnamon

1 tablespoon coconut oil (can sub for grass-fed butter), melted

3 tablespoons coconut milk

1 large egg

1–2 tablespoons nondairy chocolate chips

Vanilla mug cake can be made in the oven. Preheat to 350°F (180°C) and follow instructions as above, but bake for 10–12 minutes, or until a toothpick comes out "just" clean.

1. In a small bowl, combine the dry ingredients and mix well.

2. In a medium-sized bowl, combine the melted coconut oil, coconut milk, and egg and whisk well.

3. Combine the wet and dry ingredients and mix until a batter remains. Transfer to a greased microwave-safe mug or small bowl. Top with chocolate chips and microwave for 1–2 minutes, or until just cooked.

FLOURLESS KETO PEANUT BUTTER COOKIES

The classic peanut butter cookie has been given a keto makeover! Made with peanut butter, eggs, and a granulated sweetener of your choice, take it up a notch by adding some sugar-free chocolate chips.

Yield: 15 cookies | **Total time:** 10–12 minutes

NUTRITIONAL INFORMATION PER COOKIE

Calories 130, Protein 4 grams, Fat 9 grams, Fiber 3 grams, Carbs 6 grams, Net Carbs 2.8 grams

1 cup smooth peanut butter

1 large egg

½ cup granulated sweetener of choice

¼ cup nondairy chocolate chips (optional)

Cookies can keep at room temperature, in a sealed container, for up to a week.

1. Preheat the oven to 350°F (180°C). Line a large baking tray with parchment paper and set aside.

2. In a large mixing bowl, combine the peanut butter, egg, and sweetener and mix very well. A thick batter should remain.

3. Using your hands, roll the dough into 15 small balls. Place on the lined baking tray. Using a fork, press each ball into a cookie shape. Top with chocolate chips and bake for 10–12 minutes, or until cookies are "just" cooked. Remove from the oven and allow to cool on the pan for 10 minutes before transferring to a wire rack to cool completely.

EASY KETO OATMEAL

Enjoy this classic breakfast staple with a keto makeover!
Have it warm or overnight style (chilled overnight in a refrigerator).
The best part? You can batch-prep it.

Yield: 1 serving | **Total time:** 5 minutes

NUTRITIONAL INFORMATION
Calories 301, Protein 10 grams, Fat 19 grams, Fiber 18 grams, Carbs 20 grams, Net Carbs 2 grams

2 tablespoons ground flaxseed meal

2 tablespoons chia seeds

2 tablespoons unsweetened shredded coconut

2 tablespoons granulated sweetener of choice

½ cup hot liquid of choice

½ cup cold liquid of choice

Toppings of choice

Oatmeal can be prepped in advance or can be bulk-made.

Oatmeal can be enjoyed overnight style. Simply prepare it as described in the recipe instructions, but add an extra 2 to 3 tablespoons of liquid before placing it in the refrigerator.

1. In a small mixing bowl, combine all the dry ingredients.

2. Add the hot liquid of choice and mix well—it should be incredibly thick. Add the cold liquid of choice and mix until a thick and creamy oatmeal-like texture remains.

3. Add toppings of choice and enjoy!

KETO PIZZA CRUST

A low-carb, high-fiber pizza crust made with no eggs and no yeast? You bet! Make a few extra so that you'll have crusts on hand for quick and easy pizzas anytime.

Yield: 4 servings | **Total time** 15--20 minutes

NUTRITIONAL INFORMATION PER SERVING

Calories 130, Protein 3 grams, Fat 7 grams, Fiber 13 grams, Carbs 15 grams, Net Carbs 2 grams

¾ cup coconut flour, sifted

¼ teaspoon sea salt

½ teaspoon mixed spices of choice (I use basil, chives, and red pepper flakes)

2 tablespoons ground psyllium husks

1 tablespoon avocado oil (can sub for olive oil)

1 cup warm water (not boiling)

These pizza crusts can be made in advance for future use. To freeze, wrap each crust individually in parchment paper. Thaw completely before cooking with the toppings.

1. Preheat the oven to 400°F (200°C). Line a large tray with parchment paper and set aside.

2. In a large mixing bowl, combine all the ingredients and mix very well. Using your hands, knead the dough for 2 to 3 minutes, pressing it together to combine. The batter may seem a little wet, but it will slowly become firmer as the moisture gets more absorbed.

3. Allow the dough to sit for 15 minutes. The moisture will continue to soak up during this time.

4. Roll the dough into a pizza shape, keeping the dough around half an inch thick.

5. Top each crust with pizza sauce and toppings of choice. Bake for 12 to 15 minutes, or until the toppings have cooked and the edges of the crust are slightly brown.

6. Cool briefly and slice and enjoy!

KETO COCONUT CUPS

These cups are the easiest way to satisfy your sweet tooth—you only need two ingredients to make these coconut cups. They are the perfect snack between meals to keep hunger at bay!

Yield: 12 cups | **Total time:** 10 minutes

NUTRITIONAL INFORMATION PER CUP

Calories 238, Protein 2 grams, Fat 24 grams, Fiber N/A, Carbs 4 grams, Net Carbs 4 grams

2 cups sugar-free chocolate chips of choice, divided

1 cup coconut butter (see note)

You can substitute the coconut butter with any nut or seed butter.

1. Line a 12-count muffin tray with muffin liners and lightly grease each one.

2. In a small microwave-safe bowl or in a small pan on the stove over low heat, melt 1½ cups of the chocolate chips and fill each muffin cup three-quarters of the way, scraping down the edges to ensure it is coated. Refrigerate for 10 minutes, or until the chocolate has firmed up.

3. Be sure your coconut butter is smooth and creamy. If it is a little stiff, let the jar sit in a bowl of hot water. Do not microwave, as it will likely become dry and clumpy.

4. Drizzle the coconut butter into each of the chocolate cups. Refrigerate again for approximately 20 minutes.

5. Melt the remaining ½ cup chocolate chips and top each muffin cup with it before allowing it to firm up completely, about 30 minutes.

KETO ENGLISH MUFFIN

Satisfy your bread cravings with this two-minute keto English muffin! Don't have a microwave? No worries. This recipe comes with a tested oven option too!

Yield: 1 muffin | **Total time:** 2 minutes

NUTRITIONAL INFORMATION
Calories 327, Protein 12 grams, Fat 31 grams, Fiber 3 grams, Carbs 7 grams, Net Carbs 4 grams

3 tablespoons almond flour
½ tablespoon coconut flour
Pinch sea salt
½ teaspoon baking powder
1 tablespoon coconut oil, melted (see note)
1 large egg

Coconut oil can be substituted with melted butter.

1. In a microwave-safe bowl or ramekin (I use a ceramic cereal bowl), combine the dry ingredients and mix well.

2. Add the melted coconut oil and egg and whisk until a dough is formed.

3. Microwave for 1 to 2 minutes, or until a skewer comes out "just clean" from the center.

4. Slice in half, toast, and top with toppings of choice.

5. To make this in an oven, prepare muffin in an oven-safe ramekin (I use an 8-inch bowl) and bake in the preheated oven for 10–12 minutes, at 350°F (180°C).

READERS' FAVORITES

BEST HEALTHY
CHOCOLATE CHIP COOKIES

These are the best-tasting, healthy chocolate chip cookies you'll ever make—soft, chewy, and ready in 20 minutes! Made and loved by over 10,000 readers.

Yield: 12 cookies | **Total time:** 15 minutes

NUTRITIONAL INFORMATION
Calories 118, Protein 4 grams, Fat 12 grams, Fiber 2 grams, Carbs 12

2 cups almond flour (I used blanched almond flour)

1 teaspoon baking powder

¼ cup arrowroot starch (can sub for cornstarch)

2 tablespoons coconut oil

6 tablespoons pure maple syrup (can sub for agave nectar)

1 teaspoon vanilla extract

¼ cup milk of choice

½ cup chocolate chips of choice

Cookies can be stored at room temperature, in an airtight container for up to 1 week. They can also be refrigerated and freeze well.

1. Preheat the oven to 350°F. Line a baking tray with parchment paper and set aside.

2. In a large mixing bowl, add all your dry ingredients and mix well.

3. In a microwave-safe bowl or using a saucepan on the stove, melt the coconut oil with the syrup and vanilla extract. Add to the dry mixture, along with your milk of choice, and mix very well. Stir through the chocolate chips.

4. Lightly wet your hands and form small balls out of the cookie dough. Place the balls on the lined cookie sheet. Press each ball into a cookie shape. Bake for 12 to 15 minutes, or until just golden brown.

5. Remove from the oven and allow cookies to cool on the pan completely.

FOOL-PROOF 2-INGREDIENT FUDGE

Satisfy your chocolate and fudge craving in one, with this easy, two-ingredient fudge. Ready in 5 minutes, it's customizable and has no dairy or condensed milk.

Yield: 20 pieces | **Total time:** 5 minutes

NUTRITIONAL INFORMATION
Calories 102, Protein 2 grams, Fat 8 grams, Fiber, 1 gram, Carbs 8

1 cup chocolate chips of choice

½ cup smooth almond butter (can sub for any smooth nut or seed butter)

Fudge should be kept refrigerated at all times. It is freezer-friendly and can be enjoyed directly from there.

1. Line a small square pan or loaf pan with parchment paper and set aside.

2. In a microwave-safe bowl or using a small saucepan over the stove, combine your chocolate chips with your almond butter and melt until combined.

3. Pour the melted chocolate fudge mixture in the lined pan. Refrigerate for around 30 minutes, or until firm. Cut into pieces and enjoy!

NO-BAKE CHERRY COCONUT CANDY BARS

Inspired by the popular Cherry Ripe candy bar, this home-made version is easy and delicious. Much healthier than store-bought bars, it is the perfect dessert or even holiday gift.

Yield: 20 squares | **Total time:** 15 minutes

NUTRITIONAL INFORMATION
Calories 228, Protein 2 grams, Fat 14 grams, Fiber 2 grams, Carbs 26

3 cups finely shredded unsweetened coconut

1 cup dried cherries

½ cup granulated sweetener of choice

1⅓ cups condensed coconut milk (can sub for traditional condensed milk)

2 cups chocolate chips of choice

While these bars are stable at room temperature, they are best kept refrigerated.

1. In a high-speed blender or food processor, combine the shredded unsweetened coconut with the dried cherries and blend until a crumbly consistency remains.

2. Transfer to a large mixing bowl. Add your granulated sweetener of choice and mix well. Add the coconut condensed milk and mix until a thick batter remains. If the batter is too gooey or wet, add a little extra coconut.

3. Pour the batter into a lined 8-inch square pan or small loaf pan. Refrigerate or freeze until firm. Once firm, cut into 12 bars and refrigerate.

4. In a medium microwave-safe bowl or in a small pan on the stove over low heat, melt the chocolate chips.

5. Remove the cherry coconut bars from the fridge. Using two forks, dip each bar in the melted chocolate until evenly coated. Repeat until all the bars are covered.

6. Refrigerate until the chocolate has firmed up.

COCONUT MILK CHOCOLATE ICE CREAM

No one needs an ice cream maker to satisfy their chocolate ice cream cravings. You only need three ingredients to make this smooth and creamy chocolate coconut milk ice cream!

Yield: 8 small scoops | **Total time:** 5 minutes, plus 4 hours to freeze

NUTRITIONAL INFORMATION
Calories 140, Protein 2 grams, Fat 12 grams, Fiber 1 grams, Carbs 11

1 (14-ounce) can full fat coconut milk, chilled
6 tablespoons cocoa powder
¼ cup pure maple syrup

If your ice cream becomes too icy, you can re-blend it and enjoy it soft serve style.

1. Place a freezer-safe container in the freezer and allow to chill.

2. In a high-speed blender, combine all your ingredients and blend until creamy and smooth.

3. Remove the freezer-safe container and pour the ice cream mixture into it. Allow to freeze for 4 hours, or until firm.

4. Remove from the freezer and allow to thaw for 10 to 15 minutes, before scooping into bowls.

3-INGREDIENT PEANUT BUTTER NO-BAKE BITES

Peanut butter lovers rejoice! These no-bake bites are a cross between fudge and candy, and taste like the filling of the famous peanut butter cups.

Yield: 40 bites | **Total time:** 5 minutes

NUTRITIONAL INFORMATION
Calories 101, Protein 3 grams, Fat 7 grams, Fiber 2 grams, Carbs 9

2 cups smooth peanut butter
$^2/_3$ cups pure maple syrup (can sub for agave nectar)
1 cup coconut flour

Peanut butter balls should be kept refrigerated at all times. They can keep for up to 4 weeks. They can also be frozen, for up to 2 months.

1. Line a large plate with parchment paper and set aside.

2. In a large mixing bowl, combine your peanut butter with your pure maple syrup and mix well.

3. Sift through your coconut flour and mix until a thick dough remains. If the batter is too thin, add extra coconut flour.

4. Allow batter to sit for 5 minutes, before forming small balls. Place on the lined plate and refrigerate until firm.

SWEET AND SALTY ENERGY BITES

The perfect energy boost before or after a workout that takes only minutes to whip up. Naturally sweetened and ready in minutes, it's the perfect balance of sweet with a touch of salty.

Yield: 30–40 balls, depending on size | **Total time:** 5 minutes

NUTRITIONAL INFORMATION
Calories 45, Protein 2 grams, Fat 2 grams, Fiber 1 grams, Carbs 7

1 cup Medjool dates
1¼ cups almond butter (can sub for any nut or seed butter)
1 cup mixed salted nuts of choice (I used walnuts, cashews, and almonds)

Energy bites can keep at room temperature but are best refrigerated. They last for up to 4 weeks. They are freezer friendly and can keep for up to 2 months.

1. Line plate with parchment paper and set aside.

2. In a high-speed blender or food processor, add your ingredients and blend until a thick dough remains. Ensure you regularly scrape down the sides.

3. Transfer the dough to a large mixing bowl. Using your hands, roll small balls and place on the lined plate. Once all the dough has been used up, refrigerate for 30 minutes, or until firm.

EDIBLE COOKIE DOUGH

Ever feel like digging into a bowl of raw cookie dough?
Well, here we go! Raw, edible, eggless cookie dough in a small-batch
serving so you won't go overboard. Made with wholesome ingredients and ready in minutes.

Yield: 6 servings | **Total time:** 10 minutes

NUTRITIONAL INFORMATION
Calories 255, Protein 5 grams, Fat 18
grams, Fiber 4 grams, Carbs 18

1 cup blanched almond flour

¼ cup coconut flour

¼ cup pure maple syrup

½ teaspoon vanilla extract

3 tablespoons coconut oil, melted

¼ cup chocolate chips of choice

*Leftover cookie dough can be kept
refrigerated, in a sealed container. If
you choose to eat it later in the day, it
is safe to keep at room temperature.*

1. In a small mixing bowl, combine the
    almond flour and coconut flour and mix
    well.

2. Add the maple syrup, vanilla extract,
    and melted coconut oil and mix until a
    crumbly texture remains. Add the choc-
    olate chips and continue mixing until it
    resembles cookie dough.

TRAIL MIX BARS

All the best parts of trail mix in a soft and chewy energy bar. A quick and easy snack or even quick breakfast choice.

Yield: 12 Bars | **Total time:** 15 minutes

NUTRITIONAL INFORMATION

Calories 210, Protein 3 grams, Fat 8 grams, Fiber 3 grams, Carbs 35

1¼ cups Medjool dates

½ cup raw cashews

¼ cup raw almonds

¼ cup raw walnuts

½ cup chocolate chips of choice, divided

¼ cup mix-ins of choice (dried fruit, seeds, etc.)

Bars can keep at room temperature, for up to 1 week, in a sealed container. They are also freezer friendly.

1. In a large bowl, add your pitted dates. Cover with 2 cups warm water and let sit for 10 minutes. Drain and pat dry to remove excess liquid.

2. Line an 8-inch square baking dish with parchment paper and set aside.

3. In a high-speed blender or food processor, add your cashews, almonds, and walnuts and blend until a crumbly texture remains. Do not over blend.

4. Add your softened dates and blend well, regularly scraping down the sides to ensure the mixture is fully incorporated.

5. Add 2 to 3 tablespoons of your chocolate chips and your mix-ins of choice and blend once more until just combined.

6. Transfer the trail mix bliss bar batter to the lined baking dish and press firmly in place. Refrigerate.

7. Once bars are firm, cut into eight pieces. Melt your remaining chocolate chips and drizzle over the bars.

HOMEMADE CRUNCHY BARS

A low-carb and refined sugar–free twist on the popular crunchy candy bar. Loaded with nuts and seeds, these are a game-changer dessert ready in minutes.

Yield: 24 pieces | **Total time:** 15 minutes

NUTRITIONAL INFORMATION

Calories 290, Protein 7 grams, Fat 22 grams, Fiber 4 grams, Carbs 19

1½ cups chocolate chips of choice

1 cup smooth almond butter (can sub for any nut or seed butter)

½ cup pure maple syrup (can sub for agave nectar)

¼ cup coconut oil

3 cups nuts and seeds of choice

Bars should be kept refrigerated and will keep for up to 2 weeks. They are also freezer-friendly for up to 2 months.

1. Line an 8-inch square baking dish with parchment paper and set aside.

2. In a large mixing bowl, add the nuts and seeds and set aside.

3. In a microwave-safe bowl or a small saucepan, combine your combine the chocolate chips, almond butter, maple syrup, and coconut oil and heat until melted.

4. Pour over the nuts and seeds and mix very well, until fully incorporated.

5. Pour the crunch bar batter in the lined baking dish. Refrigerate until firm, before slicing into bars.

UN-BAKED BROWNIES

Imagine, brownies that don't need an oven to whip up! These raw, un-baked brownies that are healthy enough to eat for breakfast.

Yield: 12 servings | **Total time:** 15 minutes

NUTRITIONAL INFORMATION

Calories 244, Protein 4 grams, Fat 9 grams, Fiber 5 grams, Carbs 40

¾ cups raw almonds

¼ cup mixed nuts of choice

1½ cups Medjool dates

¼ cup cocoa powder

1–2 cups chocolate chips of choice, divided

Leftover brownies can be kept refrigerated, in a sealed container. If you choose to eat it later in the day, it is safe to keep at room temperature.

1. Line a square pan with baking paper and set aside.

2. In a high-speed blender or food processor, add the nuts and blend until a crumbly texture remains.

3. Add the Medjool dates and cocoa powder and blend for 5 to 7 minutes, regularly scraping down the sides, until a thick batter remains.

4. Add half the chocolate chips and blend once more.

5. Transfer the raw brownie batter into the lined pan. Press firmly in place. Refrigerate.

6. Melt the remaining chocolate chips and pour over the top of the brownies. Once it has firmed up, slice into bars.

SUGAR-FREE CANDIED PECANS

Candied nuts minus the sugar? I promise that it isn't an impossibility! This quick and easy recipe is perfect for the holidays and even as a snack with your favorite beverage.

Yield: 12 ¼-cup servings | **Total time:** 15 minutes

NUTRITIONAL INFORMATION
Calories 185, Protein 3 grams, Fat 20 grams, Fiber 2 grams, Carbs 5

1½ cups granulated sweetener of choice, divided

¼ cup water

1 teaspoon vanilla extract

1 tablespoon cinnamon

3 cups raw pecans

1. Heat a large pan or skillet on medium heat

2. When hot, add 1 cup of your granulated sweetener of choice, water, and vanilla extract and mix until fully combined. Allow to heat up, stirring occasionally.

3. When the sweetener has completely melted, add your pecans. Start to mix around the pecans in the liquid mixture, ensuring each nut is evenly coated. Continue stirring occasionally, until the sweetener begins to crystallize on the pecans. Turn the heat off.

4. Remove the pan from the stove and allow to sit for 2 to 3 minutes. Use a wooden spoon to break apart the pecans before they crystalize together.

5. Once cooled, toss the remaining half cup of granulated sweetener and cinnamon and cover in a sealed container.

FLOURLESS APPLESAUCE CHOCOLATE FUDGE MUFFINS

Gooey, fudgy, and soft chocolate muffins made with no eggs and no flour. They are loaded with chocolate flavor and with a secret ingredient: applesauce!

Yield: 12 muffins | **Total time:** 18–22 minutes

NUTRITIONAL INFORMATION
Calories 222, Protein 6 grams, Fat 14 grams, Fiber 4 grams, Carbs 21

1 cup unsweetened applesauce

1 cup smooth almond butter (can sub for any nut or seed butter)

½ cup cocoa powder

½ cup agave nectar (can sub for pure maple syrup)

1 teaspoon baking soda

¼ cup chocolate chips

Muffins should be kept refrigerated, and last for up to 3 days. They are freezer friendly, for up to 1 month.

1. Preheat the oven to 350°F. Line a 12-count muffin tray with muffin liners and set aside.

2. In a high-speed blender or food processor, add all the ingredients, except for the chocolate chips, and blend until a smooth batter remains.

3. Divide the muffin batter between the 12 muffin tins. Divide the chocolate chips evenly amongst the muffins and bake for 18 to 22 minutes, or until a toothpick comes out clean.

4. Allow the muffins to cool completely, before removing from the tin.

ACKNOWLEDGMENTS

Clean Snacks truly had a supportive army behind it.

This last year (2017–18) has been an incredibly challenging year for me—mentally, physically, and emotionally. Plenty of good things happened, but this was also a time of self-doubt, disappointment, and anger.

Even so, there have been some amazing people who have continued to stick around. Not only are they just all-around incredible people, but they were willing to taste test on a very regular basis. I am beyond fortunate to have them all in my life and I thank them all.

Ingrid Sawyer, who knew that 17 years ago we'd be here today, Tupperware full of (visually unfortunate, but tasty) baked foods, and Ziploc bags of granola. Thank you for being the constant in a world of uncertainty.

Darren Sawyer, you said granola was always intended for you to bring on your African trips . . . not sure how often that happened though!

Andria Kalliakoudis, not only do you have a heart of pure gold, but you also spat on my first book . . . *because it's a Greek tradition!!!* Thank you for being victim to questionable edibles left on your doorstep, and thank you Christian Marcus too!

Juli and Stefan Dorfschmidt, I'm sorry there is no recipe for Harzer cheese in here, but I think the fridge may have some hidden at the back. Thank you for being my very first taste testers when you were here in Melbourne and also for being cross-country taste testers in Germany. You both mean the world to me.

Paddy Djordjevic, thank you for keeping me in shape and focused amidst days of brownies and cakes, and for also being brutally honest. I'm glad at least one recipe got your seal of approval. (Those fudgy gooey brownies on page 83!). Here's to me having a body like Ryan Reynolds by book #3.

Bec Kerr, I'm sorry I pushed you into the bushes in year 11. Thank you for being on the receiving end of many kitchen failures and also for taste testing many, many recipes. No, the salted caramel slice is *not* in this book.

Justin Cleaves, thank you for being a trooper with the recipes too—I hope Bec shared the good ones with you!

Trish Lakeland—who knew a fitness class would be such a blessing? Julia Child once said, "People who love to eat are the best kind of people." Looking forward to many, many more eating adventures with you!

James Lakeland, thank you so much for sacrificing your fitness challenge to taste test multiple recipes. Seeing as you won the challenge, I take partial credit. No, really.

Natalie Thomas, thank you for your friendship, support, and for being a brain to pick when recipe ideas had gone MIA. . . . You are the crispy noodle in an Asian vegetable salad.

Sarah Wong and Suwen Ng, thank you for celebrating *Clean Sweets* in the near-empty café and making me sign your books. I expect the same fanfare with this one.

Thuy Dao, I hope one recipe in here will meet the standards of your ketchup and corn chip pairing. Thank you for always being a supportive and (never visiting) friend.

James Hughes, thank you for being the ever-present cheerleader, especially with the leap into taking *The Big Man's World* from hobby to career. Very few can call their hiring managers for their first "big guy" job their good friends.

Sophie Danner, Melbourne, New York, Hamburg, New York again, Zurich . . . it's just a matter of where next? *Le monde. Je t'aime.*

Dad, Mum, Niki, Nana: Thank you for your ever-present support!

To my amazing literary agent, MacKenzie Fraser-Bub: Thank you for having faith in book #2 and for championing me along the way. Without you, none of this would have been possible!

Ann, Michael, and the team at The Countryman Press: Here's to seeing *Clean Snacks* enjoyed by many around the world!

Finally, I want to personally thank *you*, my loyal reader.

Hands down, the best part of my job is not the recipe testing, it's not eating ugly cake that can't be photographed, and it certainly isn't accidentally dropping molasses on my sister's head (*well, maybe that one was okay*).

The best part is my daily interactions with you, and getting to know many of you from all walks of life, wherever you may be in the world. It means so much to me when you make one of my recipes, share it with those you love, send me pictures of your creations—all of it.

Without you, I wouldn't wake up every morning feeling blessed, excited, and grateful to be able to share all of this with you.

INDEX